THE NEGRO AS A SOLDIER

WRITTEN BY

Christian A. Fleetwood,

Late Sergeant-Major 4th U. S. Colored Troops,

FOR

THE NEGRO CONGRESS,

AT THE

Cotton States and International Exposition,
Atlanta, Ga.,

November 11 to November 23, 1895.

ISBN: 978-1-63923-860-6

Printed: March 2023

Published and Distributed By:
Lushena Books
607 Country Club Drive, Unit E
Bensenville, IL 60106
www.lushenabks.com

ISBN: 978-1-63923-860-6

COTTON STATES AND INTERNATIONAL EXPOSITION,
Atlanta, Ga., 1895.

COMMISSION FOR THE DISTRICT OF COLUMBIA COLORED EXHIBIT.
Jesse Lawson, Chief Commissioner.

Edward E. Cooper, Vice Chairman,
Thomas L. Jones,
W. S. Montgomery,
James H. Meriwether,
Joseph H. Stewart,
Henry E. Baker, Treasurer,
A. F. Hilyer,
Geo. Wm. Cook,
Col. Nathan Toomer,
J. E. Johnson, Secretary.

Ladies' Auxiliary Committee.

Mrs. B. K. Bruce, President,
Mrs. J. T. Layton, 1st Vice Pres.,
Mrs. A. F. Hilyer, 2d Vice Pres.,
Mrs. Jesse Lawson, Secretary,
Mrs. Charles R. Douglass, Treas.

Men's Auxiliary Committee.

David A. Clark, Chairman,

OFFICE OF THE COMMISSION,
Room 4, 609 F Street, Northwest,
Washington, D. C. August 5, 1895.

Major C. A. FLEETWOOD.

Dear Sir:—At a meeting of the Committee for the District of Columbia on National Negro Congresses at the Atlanta Exposition, held this day, you were appointed a speaker to represent the District on the subject, "Military."

Will you kindly favor us with an early notice of your acceptance?

Very respectfully,

WALTER H. BROOKS, Chairman
W. J. HOWARD,
EDWARD H. LIPSCOMBE, Sec.
Committee.

Gift of author.

THE NEGRO AS A SOLDIER.

IN THE WAR OF THE REVOLUTION.

For sixteen hundred years prior to the war between Great Britain and the Colonies, the pages of history bear no record of the Negro as a soldier. Tracing his separate history in the Revolutionary War, is a task of much difficulty, for the reason that while individual instances of valor and patriotism abound there were so few separate bodies of Negro troops, that no separate record appears to have been made. The simple fact is that the fathers as a rule enlisted men both for the Army and Navy, just as now, is only continued by the Navy, that is to say, they were assigned wherever needed, without regard to race or color. Varner's Rhode Island Battalion appears to have been the only large aggregation of Negroes in this war, though Connecticut, New York, and New Hampshire each furnished one separate company in addition to individuals scattered through their other organizations, so that ere the close of the war, there were very few brigades, regiments, or companies in which the Negro was not in evidence.

The free Negro appears to have gone in from the beginning without attracting or calling out special comment. Later, as men grew scarcer and necessity more pressing, slaves were taken in also, and then the trouble began. Those who held slaves did not care to lose them in this way. Others who had not, did not think it just the thing in a war for avowed freedom to place an actual slave in the ranks to fight. Some did not want the Negro, bond or free, to take part as a soldier in the struggle. So that in May, 1775, the Massachusetts Committee of Safety voted that thereafter only free men should be enlisted. In July, Gen. Gates issued an order prohibiting further enlistments of Negroes, but saying nothing of those already in the service.

In October, a council of war, presided over by Gen. Washington, comprising three Major Generals and six Brigadier Generals, voted unanimously against the enlistment of slaves, and by a decided majority against further enlistments of Negroes. Ten days later in a conference held at Cambridge, Mass., participated in by Gen. Washington, Benj. Franklin, Benj. Harrison, Thos. Lynch, and the deputy governors of Connecticut and Rhode Island, the same action was taken.

On the 7th November, 1775, Earl Dundore, commanding the forces of His Majesty the King, issued a proclamation offering freedom and equal pay to all slaves who would join his armies as soldiers. It did not take the the colonists long to find out their mistake, although Gen. Washington, in accordance with the expressed will of his officers and of the Committee of Safety, did on the 17th Nov., 1775, issue a proclamation forbidding the further enlistment of Negroes. Less than two months later, that is to say on the 30th Dec., 1775, he issued a second proclamation again authorizing the enlistment of free Negroes He advised Congress of his action, and stated that he would recall it if so directed. But he was not. The splendid service rendered by the Negro and the great and pressing need of men were such, that although the opposition continued from some sections, it was not thereafter strong enough to get recognition. So the Negroes went and came much as did other men.

In all the events of the war, from Bunker Hill to Yorktown, they bore an honorable part. The history of the doings of the armies is their history, as in everything they took part and did their share. Their total enlistment was about 3,000 men. A very fair percentage for the then population. I might instance the killing of Major Pitcairn, at Bunker Hill, by Peter Salem, and of Major Montgomery at Fort Griswold by Jordan Freeman. The part they took in the capture of Major-General Prescott at Newport; their gallant defense of Colonel Greene, their beloved commander, when he was surprised and murdered at Croton River, May 13, 1781, when it was only after the last of his faithful guards had been shot and cut down that he was reached; or at the battle of Rhode Island, when a battalion of 400 Negroes withstood three separate and distinct charges from 1,500 Hessians under Count Donop, and beat them back with such tremendous loss that Count Donop at once applied for an exchange, fearing that his men would kill him if he went into battle with them again, for having exposed them to such slaughter; and many other instances that are of record. The letter following, written Dec, 5, 1775, explains itself;

To the Honorable General Court of the Massachusetts Bay.

The subscribers beg leave to report to your Honorable House (which we do in justice to the character of so brave a man), that under our own observation we declare that a Negro Man named Salem Poor, of Col. Frye's Regiment, Cap. Ames' Company, in the late battle at Charleston, behaved like an experienced officer as well as an excellent soldier. To set forth particulars of his conduct would be tedious. We would only beg to say, in the person of this Negro centers a brave and gallant soldier. The reward due to so great and distinguished a character, we submit to Congress.

JONA. BREWER, Col.	WM. PRESCOTT, Col.
THOMAS NIXON, Lt. Col.	EPHM. COREY, Lieut.
JOSEPH BAKER, Lieut.	JOSHUA ROW, Lieut.
JONAS RICHARDSON, Capt.	ELIPHALETT BODWELL, Sergt.
EBENEZER VARNUM, 2 Lt.	WM. HUDSON BALLARD, Capt.
WILLIAM SMITH Capt.	JOHN MORTON, Sergt.
RICHARD WELSH, Lieut.	

This is a splendid and well attested tribute to a gallant and worthy Negro. There were many such, but, beyond receiving and reading no action was taken thereon by Congress. There is no lack of incidents and the temptation to quote many of them is great, but the time allotted me is too brief for extended mention and I must bring this branch of my subject to a close. It is in evidence that while so many Negroes were offering their lives a willing sacrifice for the country, in some sections the officers of the Continental Forces received their bounty and pay in Negroes, "grown" and "small," instead of "dollars" and "cents." Fighting for *Liberty* and taking pay in *Slaves!*

When the war was over the free men returned to meet their same difficulties; the slaves were caught when possible and reenslaved by their former masters. In Boston a few years later we find a party of black patriots of the Revolution mobbed on Boston Common while celebrating the anniversary of the abolition of the slave trade.

The captain of a vessel trading along the coast tells of a Negro who had fought in the war and been distinguished for bravery and soldierly conduct. He was reclaimed and reenslaved by his master after the war, and served him faithfully until old age rendered him useless. The master then brought the poor old slave to this captain and asked him to take him along on his trip and try to sell him. The captain hated to sell a man who had fought for his country, but finally agreed, took the poor old man to Mobile, and sold him for $100 to a man who put him to attending a chicken coop. His former master continued to draw the old slave's pension as a soldier in the Revolution, until he died.

THE WAR OF 1812.

The war of 1812 was mainly fought upon the water, and in the American navy at that time the Negro stood in the ratio of about one to six. We find record of complaint by Commodore Perry at the beginning because of the large number of Negroes sent him, but later the highest tribute to their bravery and efficiency. Capt. Shaler, of the armed brig General Thompson, writing of an engagement between his vessel and a British frigate, says :

"The name of one of my poor fellows, who was killed, ought to to be registered in the book of fame, and remembered as long as bravery is a virtue. He was a black man, by name John Johnson. A twenty-four pound shot struck him in the hip, and took away all the lower part of his body. In this state the poor brave fellow lay on the deck, and several times exclaimed to his shipmates : 'Fire away, my boys; no haul a color down!' Another black man, by the name of John Davis, who was struck in much the same manner, repeatedly requested to be thrown overboard, saying that he was only in the way of others."

I know of nothing finer in history than these.

As before, the Negro was not universally welcomed to the ranks of the American army; but later continued reverses and a lack of enthusiasm in enlistments made it necessary to seek his aid, and from Mobile, Ala., on September 21, 1814, General Jackson issued a stirring call to the free colored people of Louisiana for aid. It began thus:

"Through a mistaken policy you have heretofore been deprived of a participation in the glorious struggle for national rights in which our country is engaged. This no longer shall exist."

In a remarkably short period, two battalions were raised, under Majors LaCaste and Savary, which did splendid service in the battle of New Orleans. New York enrolled two battalions, and sent them to Sacketts Harbor. Pennsylvania enrolled twenty-four hundred, and sent them to Gray's Ferry at the capture of Washton, to prepare for the invading column. Another battalion also was raised, armed, equipped and ready to start to the front, when peace was declared.

Let us hear the testimony of that original democrat, General Jackson. Under the date of Dec. 18, 1814, he writes as follows:

"To the men of color, soldiers : From the shores of Mobile I called you to arms. I invited you to share in the perils and to divide the glory of your white countrymen. I expected much from you; for I was not uninformed of those qualities which must render you so formidable to an invading foe. I knew you could endure hunger and thirst, and all the hardships of war. I knew that you loved the land of your nativity, and that, like ourselves, you had to defend all that is most dear to man. But you surpass my hopes. I have found in you, united to those qualities, that noble enthusiasm that impels to great deeds.

"Soldiers : The President of the United States shall be informed of your conduct on the present occasion, and the voice of the representatives of the American nation shall applaud your valor, as your general now praises your ardor. The enemy is near. His sails cover the lakes, but the brave are united, and if he finds us contending among ourselves, it will be for the prize of valor, and fame its noblest reward."

In one of the actions of this war, a charging column of the American army was repulsed and thrown into great disorder. A Negro private, seeing the disaster, sprang upon a horse, and by heroic effort rallied the troops, led them back upon a second charge, and completely routed the enemy. He was rewarded by General Jackson with the honorary title of Major. Under the laws he could not commission him.

When the war was over, this gallant man returned to his home in Nashville, Tenn., where he lived for years afterward, highly respected by its citizens of all races.

At the age of seventy years, this black hero was obliged, *in self-defense*, to strike a white ruffian, who had assaulted him. Under the laws of the State he was arrested and given nine and thirty lashes on his bare back. It broke his heart, and Major Jeffreys died.

THE WAR FOR THE UNION.

It seems a little singular that in the tremendous struggle between the States in 1861-1865, the south should have been the first to take steps toward the enlistment of Negroes. Yet such is the fact. Two weeks after the fall of Fort Sumter, the "Charleston Mercury" records the passing through Augusta of several companies of the the 3rd and 4th Georgia Regt., and of sixteen well-drilled companies *and one Negro company* from Nashville, Tenn.

"The Memphis Avalanche" and "The Memphis Appeal" of

May 9, 10, and 11, 1861, give notice of the appointment by the
"Committee of Safety" of a committee of three persons "to organ-
ize a volunteer company composed of our patriotic freemen of color
of the city of Memphis, for the service of our common defense."

A telegram from New Orleans dated November 23, 1861, notes
the review by Gov. Moore of over 28,000 troops, and that one regiment comprised "*1,400 colored men.*" "The New Orleans Pica-
yune," referring to a review held February 9, 1862, says: "We
must also pay a deserved compliment to the companies of free
colored men, all very well drilled and comfortably equipped."

It is a little odd, too, that in the evacuation of New Orleans a
little later, in April, 1862, all of the troops succeeded in getting
away except the Negroes. They "got left."

It is not in the line of this paper to speculate upon what would
have been the result of the war had the South kept up this policy,
enlisted the freemen, and emancipated the enlisting slaves and
their families. The immense addition to their fighting force, the
quick recognition of them by Great Britain, to which slavery was
the greatest bar, and the fact that the heart of the Negro was with
the South but for slavery, and the case stands clear. But the
primary successes of the South closed its eyes to its only chance of
salvation, while at the same time the eyes of the North were opened.

In 1865, the South saw, and endeavored to remedy its error. On
March 9, 1865, the Confederate Congress passed a bill, recommended
by Gen. Lee, authorizing the enlistment of 200,000 Negroes; but it
was then too late.

The North came slowly and reluctantly to recognize the Negro as
a factor for good in the war. "This is a white man's war," met the
Negroes at every step of their first efforts to gain admission to the
armies of the Union.

To General David Hunter more than to any other one man, is due
the credit for the successful entry upon the stage of the Negro as a
soldier in this war.

In the spring of 1862, he raised and equipped a regiment of
Negroes in South Carolina, and when the fact became known in
Washington and throughout the country, such a storm was raised
about the ears of the administration that they gracefully stood
aside and left the brave general to fight his enemies in the front and
rear as best he might. He was quite capable to do both, as it
proved.

On the 9th of June, 1862, Mr. Wickliffe, of Kentucky, introduced a resolution in the House of Representatives, which was passed, calling upon the Secretary of War for information as to the fact of these enlistments and by what authority this matter was done.

The Secretary of War replied under date June 14, 1862, disavowing any official knowledge of such a regiment and denying that any authority had been given therefor. He referred the resolution to Gen. Hunter' His reply is one of the best things of the war I quote it entire.

Headquarters, Department of the South,

Port Royal, S. C., June 23, 1862.

Hon. Edwin M. Stanton, Secretary of War,

Washington.

SIR : I have the honor to acknowledge the receipt of a communication from the Adjutant-General of the Army, dated June 16, 1862, requesting me to furnish you with the information necessary to answer certain resolutions introduced in the House of Representatives June 9, 1862, on motion of the Hon. Mr. Wickliffe, of Kentucky, their substance being to inquire : First, whether I had organized, or was organizing, a regiment of fugitive slaves in this department; Second, whether any authority had been given to me from the War Department for such organization; and Third. whether I had been furnished by order of the War Department with clothing, uniforms, arms, equipments, etc., for such a force.

Only having received the letter conveying the inquiries at a late hour on Saturday night, I urge forward my answer in time for the steamer sailing to-day (Monday), this haste preventing me from entering as minutely as I could wish upon many points of detail, such as the paramount importance of the subject calls for. But in view of the near termination of the present session of Congress, and the widespread interest which must have been awakened by Mr. Wickliffe's resolution, I prefer sending even this imperfect answer to waiting the period necessary for the collection of fuller and more comprehensive data.

To the first question, therefore, I reply that no regiment of "fugitive slaves" has been or is organized in this department. There is, however, a fine regiment of persons whose late masters are "fugitive rebels," men who everywhere fly before the appearance of the national flag, leaving their servants behind them to shift as best they can for themselves. So far, indeed, are the loyal persons composing this regiment from seeking to avoid the presence of their late owners that they are now, one and all, working with remarkable industry to place themselves in a position to go in full and effective pursuit of their fugacious and traitorous proprietors.

To the second question, I have the honor to answer, that the instructions given to Brig.-General W. T. Sherman by the Hon. Simon Cameron, late Secretary of War, and turned over to me by succession for my guidance, do distinctly authorize me to employ all loyal persons offering their services in defense of the Union and for the suppression of this rebellion in any manner I might see fit, or that the circumstances might call for. There is no restriction as to the character or color of the persons who might be employed, or the nature of the employment; whether civil or military, in which their services should be used. I conclude, therefore, that I have been authorized to enlist "fugitive slaves" as soldiers, could any be found in this department.

No such characters have, however, yet appeared within our most advanced pickets, the loyal slaves everywhere remaining on their plantations to welcome us, and supply us with food, labor and information. It is the masters who have, in every instance, been the "fugitives"—running away from loyal slaves as well as loyal soldiers, and whom we have only partially been able to see—chiefly their heads over ramparts, or, rifle in hand, dodging behind trees, in the extreme distance. In the absence of any "fugitive master" law, the deserted slaves would be wholly without remedy, had not the crime of treason given them the right to pursue, capture, and bring back those persons of whose protection they have been thus suddenly bereft.

To the third interrogatory, it is my painful duty to reply, that I never have received any specific authority for issues of clothing, uniforms, arms, equipments, etc., to the troops in question. My general instructions from Mr. Cameron, to employ them in any manner I might find necessary, and the military exigencies of the department and the country being my only, but, in my judgment, sufficient justification. Neither have I had any specific authority for supplying these persons with shovels, spades and pickaxes when employing them as laborers, nor with boats and oars when using them as lightermen; but these are not points included in Mr. Wickliffe's resolution. To me it seemed that liberty to employ men in any particular capacity implied with it liberty also to supply them with the necessary tools; and acting under this faith I have clothed, equipped and armed the only loyal regiment yet raised in South Carolina.

I must say in vindication of my conduct that had it not been for the many other diversified and imperative claims on my time, a much more satisfactory result might have been hoped for; and that, in place of only one, as at present, at least five or six well-drilled, brave, and thoroughly acclimated regiments should by this time have been added to the loyal forces of the Union.

The experiment of arming the blacks, so far as I have made it, has been a complete and even marvellous success. They are sober, docile, attentive, and enthusiastic, displaying great natural capacities for acquiring the duties of a soldier. They are eager beyond all things to take the field and be led into action; and it is the unanimous opinion of the officers who have had charge of them, that in the peculiarities of this climate and country, they will prove invaluable auxiliaries, fully equal to the similar regiments so long and successfully used by the British authorities in the West Indies.

In conclusion I would say it is my hope, there appearing to be no possibility of other reinforcements owing to the exigencies of the campaign in the peninsular, to have organized by the end of next fall and to be able to present to the Government from forty-eight to fifty thousand of these hardy and devoted soldiers.

Trusting that this letter may form part of your answer to Mr. Wickliffe's resolution.

I have the honor to be, most respectfully, your obedient servant,

D. HUNTER,
Major General Commanding.

The reading of this famous document in the House brought out such a storm of laughter, from both friends and foes that further action was impossible. The Hon. Sunset Cox speaking of the matter some years later said : "I tell you that letter from Hunter spoiled the prettiest speech I had ever thought of making. I had been delighted with Wickliffe's motion, and thought the reply to it would furnish us with first-rate democratic thunder for the next election. I made up my mind to sail in on Hunter's answer no matter what it was—the moment it came, and to be even more humorously successful in its delivery and reception than I was in my speech against war-horse Gurley of Ohio. Well you see, man proposes, but Providence orders otherwise. When the clerk announced the receipt of the letter, and that he was about to read it, I caught the Speaker's eye, and was booked for the first speech against your Negro experiment. The first sentence being formal and official was very well : but at the second the House began to grin, and at the third, there was not a man on the floor, except Father Wickliffe, of Kentucky, perhaps, who was not convulsed with laughter. Even my own risibles I found to be affected, and before the document was concluded, I motioned to the Speaker that he might give the floor to whom he pleased, as my desire to distinguish myself in in that particular tilt was over.''

The beginning of 1863, saw the opening of the doors to the Negro in every direction. General Lorenzo Thomas went in person to the valley of the Mississippi to supervise it there   Massachusetts was authorized to fill its quota with Negroes.   The States of Maryland, Missouri, Delaware and Tennesee were thrown open by order of the War Department, and all slaves enlisting therefrom declared free   Ohio, Connecticut, Pennsylvania and New York joined the band and sent the stalwart black boy in blue to the front singing, "Give us a flag, all free, without a slave." For two years the fierce and determined opposition had kept them out, but now the bars were down and they came pouring in. Some one said he cared not who made the laws of a people if he could make their songs. A better exemplification of this would be difficult to find than is the song written by "Miles O'Reilly" (Col. Halpine), of the old 10th Army Corps. I cannot resist the temptation to quote it here. With General Hunter's letter and this song to quote from, the episode was closed:

Some say it is a burning shame to make the Naygurs fight,
    An' that the trade o' being kilt belongs but to the white:
But as for me, upon me sowl, so liberal are we here,
    I'll let Sambo be murthered, in place of meself, on every day of the year.
On every day of the year, boys, and every hour in the day,
    The right to be kilt I'll divide wid him, and divil a word I'll say.

In battles wild commotion I shouldn't at all object,
    If Sambo's body should stop a ball that was coming for me direct,
An' the prod of a southern bayonet, so liberal are we here,
    I'll resign and let Sambo take it, on every day in the year,
On every day in the year, boys, an' wid none of your nasty pride,
    All right in a southern bagnet prod, wid Sambo I'll divide.

The men who object to Sambo, should take his place and fight,
    An' it is betther to have a Naygur's hue, than a liver that's weak an' white,
Though Sambo's black as the ace of spades, his finger a thryger can pull,
    An' his eye runs straight on the barrel sight from under its thatch of wool,
So hear me all, boys, darlin, don't think I'm tipping you chaff,
    The right to be kilt, I'll divide with him, an' give him the largest half.

It took three years of war to place the enlisted Negro upon the same ground as the enlisted white man as to pay and emoluments: *perhaps* six years of war might have given him shoulder-straps, but the war ended without authorization of law for that step. At first they were received, under an act of Congress that allowed each one, without regard to rank, ten dollars per month, three dollars thereof to be retained for clothing and equipments. I think it was in May, '64, when the act was passed equalizing the pay, but not opening the doors to promotion.

Under an act of the Confederate Congress, making it a crime punishable with death for any white person to train any Negro or mulatto to arms, or aid them in any military enterprise, and devoting the Negro caught under arms to the tender mercies of the "present or future laws of the State" in which caught, a large number of *promotions* were made by the way of a rope and a tree along the first year of the Negro's service (I can even recall one instance as late as April 1865, though it had been long before then generally discontinued).

What the Negro did, how he did it, and where, it would take volumes to properly record, I can however give but briefest mention to a few of the many evidences of his fitness for the duties of the war, and his aid to the cause of the Union.

The first fighting done by organized Negro troops appears to have been done by Company A, First South Carolina Negro Regiment, at St. Helena Island, November 3–10, 1862, while participating in an expedition along the coast of Georgia and Florida under Lt.-Col. O. T. Beard, of the Forty-eighth New York Infantry, who says in his report:—

"The colored men fought with astonishing coolness and bravery. I found them all I could desire, more than I had hoped. They behaved gloriously, and deserve all praise."

The testimony thus inaugurated runs like a cord of gold through the web and woof of the history of the Negro as a soldier from that date to their final charge, the last made at Clover Hill, Va., April 9, 1865.

Necessarily the first actions in which the Negro bore a part commanded most attention. Friends and enemies were looking eagerly to see how they would acquit themselves, and so it comes to pass that the names of Fort Wagner, Olustee, Millikens Bend, Port Hudson and Fort Pillow are as familiar as Bull Run, Antietam, Shiloh and Gettysburg, and while those first experiences were mostly severe reverses, they were by that very fact splendid exemplifiers of the truth that the Negroes could be relied upon to fight under the most adverse circumstances, against any odds, and could not be discouraged.

Let us glance for a moment at Port Hudson, La., in May, 1863, assaulted by General Banks with a force of which the First and Second Regiments, Louisiana Native Guards, formed a part. When starting upon their desperate mission, Colonel Stafford of the First Regiment in turning over the regimental, colors to the color guard, made a brief and patriotic address, closing in the words:

"Color Guard: Protect, defend, die for, but do not surrender these colors." The gallant flag-sergeant, Plancianos, taking them replied: "Colonel: I will bring back these colors to you in honor, or report to God the reason why."

Six times with desperate valor they charged over ground where success was hopeless, a deep bayou between them and the works of the enemy at the point of attack rendered it impossible to reach them, yet strange to say, six times they were ordered forward and six times they went to useless death, until swept back by the blazing breath of shot and shell before which nothing living could stand. Here fell the gallant Captain Cailloux, black as the ace of spades; refusing to leave the field though his arm had been shattered by a bullet he returned to the charge until killed by a shell.

A soldier limping painfully to the front was halted and asked where he was going, he replied; "I am shot bad in de leg, and dey want me to go to de hospital, but I guess I can give 'em a little more yet."

The colors came back but crimsoned with the blood of the gallant Plancianos, who reported to God from that bloody field.

Shall we glance from this to Millikens Bend, La., in January, 1863, garrisoned by the Ninth and Eleventh Louisiana and the First Mississippi, all Negroes, and about one hundred and sixty of the twenty-third Iowa (white), about eleven hundred fighting men in all. Attacked by a force of six Confederate regiments, crushed out of their works by sheer weight of numbers, borne down toward the levee, fighting every step of the way, hand to hand, clubbed musket, bayonets and swords, from three a. m. to twelve, noon, when a Union gun-boat came to the rescue and shelled the desperate foe back to the woods, with a total loss to the defenders of 437 men, two-fifths of their strength.

Shall we turn with sadness to Fort Wagner, S. C., in July, 1863, when the Fifty-fourth Mass. won its deathless fame, and its grand young commander, Col. Robert Gould Shaw, passed into the temple of immortality. After a march of all day, under a burning sun, and all night through a tempest of wind and rain, drenched, exhausted, hungry, they wheel into line, without a murmur for that awful charge, that dance of death, the struggle against hopeless odds, and the shattered remnants were hurled back as from the mouth of hell, leaving the dead bodies of their young commander and his noble followers to be buried in a common grave. Its total loss was about one-third of its strength.

Here it was that the gallant Flag-sergeant Carney, though grievously wounded, bore back his flag to safety, and fell fainting and exhausted with loss of blood, saying, "Boys, the old flag never touched the ground!" Or another glance, at ill-starred Olustee, where the gallant 8th U. S. C. T. lost 87 killed of its effective fighting force, the largest loss in any one colored regiment in any one action of the war. And so on, by Fort Pillow, which let us pass in merciful silence, and to Honey Hill, S. C., perhaps the last desperate fight in the far south, in which the 32nd, 35th and 102nd U. S. C. T. and the 54th and 55th Mass. Inf. won fresh and fadeless laurels for splendid fighting against hopeless odds and insurmountable difficulties, and then to Nashville, Tennessee, with its recorded loss of 84 killed in the effectives of the 13th U. S. C. T.

These were all brilliant actions, and they covered the actors with and reflected upon the race a blaze of glory. But it was in the armies of the James and of the Potomac that the true metal of the Negro as a soldier rang out its clearest notes amid the tremendous diapasons that rolled back and forth between the embattled hosts. Here was war indeed, upon its grandest scale, and in all its infinite variety. The tireless march under burning sun, chilling frosts and driven tempests, the lonely vigil of the picket under starless skies, the rush and roar of countless "hosts to battle driven" in the mad charge and the victorious shout that pursued the fleeing foe;

the grim determination that held its line of defenses with set teeth, blood-shot eye and strained muscle beating back charge after charge of the foe; the patient labor in trench and mine, on hill and in valley, swamp and jungle, with disease adding its horrors to the decimation of shot and shell.

Here the Negro stood in the full glare of the greatest search light, part and parcel of the grandest armies ever mustered upon this continent, competing side by side with the best and bravest of the Union army against the flower of the Confederacy, the best and bravest of Lee's army, and losing nothing in the contrast. Never again while time lasts will the doubt arise as in 1861, "Will the Negro fight?" As a problem, it has been solved, as a question it has been answered, and as a fact it is as established as the eternal hills. It was they who rang up the curtain upon the last act of the bloody tragedy at Petersburg, Va., June 15, 1864, and they who rang it down at Clover Hill, Va., April 9, 1865. They were one of the strong fingers upon the mighty hand that grasped the giant's throat at Petersburg and never flexed until the breath went out at Appomattox. In this period it would take page on page to recount their deeds of valor and their glorious victories.

See them on the 15th of June, 1864, carrying the outpost at Baylor's field in early morning, and all that long, hot, summer day advancing, a few yards at a time, then lying down to escape the fire from the works, but still gradually creeping nearer and nearer, until, just as the sun went down, they swept like a tornado over the works and started upon a race for the city, close at the heels of the flying foe, until mistakenly ordered back. Of this day's experience Gen. Badeau writes: "No worse strain on the nerves of troops is possible, for it is harder to remain quiet under cannon fire, even though comparatively harmless, than to advance against a storm of musketry." General W. F. "Baldy" Smith, speaking of their conduct, says: "No nobler effort has been put forth to-day, and no greater success achieved than that of the colored troops."

In his order of the day he says:

"To the colored troops comprising the Division of General Hinks, the general commanding would call the attention of his command. With the veterans of the Eighteenth corps, they have stormed the works of the enemy and carried them, taking guns and prisoners, and in the whole affair they have displayed all the qualities of good soldiers."

Or, again, at the terrible mine explosion of July 30, 1864, on the Petersburg line, and at the fearful slaughter of September 29, 1864, at New Market Heights and Fort Harrison. On this last date in the Fourth U. S. Col. Troops, out of a color-guard of twelve men, but one came off the field on his own feet. The gallant Flag-sergeant Hilton, the last to fall, cried out as he went down, "Boys, save the colors;" and they were saved.

After the magnificent fighting of this last date, under date of Oct. 11, 1864, Maj.-General B. F. Butler issued an order, a portion of which I quote, as follows:

"Of the colored soldiers of the third divisions of the 18th and 10th Corps and the officers who led them, the general commanding desires to make special mention. In the charge on the enemy's works by the colored division of the 18th Corps at New Market, better men were never better led, better officers never led better men. A few more such gallant charges and to command colored troops will be the post of honor in the American armies. The colored soldiers, by coolness, steadiness, determined courage and dash, have silenced every cavil of the doubters of their soldierly capacity, and drawn tokens of admiration from their enemies, have brought their late masters even to the consideration of the question whether they will not employ as soldiers the hitherto despised race."

Some ten or more years later, in Congress, in the midst of a speech advocating the giving of civil rights to the Negro, Gen. Butler said, referring to this incident:

"There, in a space not wider than the clerk's desk, and three hundred yards long, lay the dead bodies of 543 of my colored comrades, slain in the defense of their country, who had laid down their lives to uphold its flag and its honor, as a willing sacrifice. And as I rode along, guiding my horse this way and that, lest he should profane with his hoofs what seemed to me the sacred dead, and as I looked at their bronzed faces upturned in the shining sun, as if in mute appeal against the wrongs of the country for which they had given their lives, and whose flag had been to them a flag of stripes, in which no star of glory had ever shone for them.—feeling I had wronged them in the past, and believing what was the future duty of my country to them— I swore to myself a solemn oath: 'May my right hand forget its cunning, and my tongue cleave to the roof of my mouth, if ever I fail to defend the rights of the men who have given their blood for me and my country this day and for their race forever. And, God helping me, I will keep that oath.'"

Or another instance : when under Butler first and Terry later, driven by storms and tempestous seas to powerful Fort Fisher, cooperating with our gallant Navy in its capture, and thence starting on the long march that led through Wilmington, and on to Goldsboro, N. C., where Johnson's army, the last large force of the Confederacy in the field, was caught between the forces under Terry and the forces under Howard; and the war as such was ended with his surrender, April 26, 1865.

A little of statistics, and I will close.

The total number of colored soldiers in this last war was 178,975, and the number of deaths 36,847.

Of enlistments the United States made 96,337, and the several States 79,638.

Enlistments were divided as follows :

Alabama	2,969	Mississippi	17,869
Louisiana	24,052	Maine	104
New Hampshire	125	Vermont	120
Massachusetts	3,966	Rhode Island	1,837
Connecticut	1,764	New York	4,125
New Jersey	1,185	Pennsylvania	8,612
Delaware	954	Maryland	8,718
Dist. of Columbia	3,269	Virginia	5,723
North Carolina	5,035	West Virginia	196
South Carolina	5,462	Georgia	3,486
Florida	1,044	Arkansas	5,526
Tennessee	20,133	Kentucky	23,703
Michigan	1,387	Ohio	5,092
Indiana	1,537	Illinois	1,811
Missouri	8,344	Minnesota	104
Iowa	440	Wisconsin	165
Kansas	2,080	Texas	47
Colorado Ter.	95	Miscellaneous	5,896

The completed organizations were as follows :

138 regiments of infantry.
6   "   " cavalry.
14   "   " heavy artillery.
1   "   " light artillery.

On 449 occasions their blood was spilled.

These are a few of the regiments having the largest number of men killed in any one engagement.

The 8th U. S. C. T., at Olustee, 87 killed.
" 13th " Nashville, 84 "
" 23rd " Petersburg, 81
" 7th " Fort Gilmore, 68
" 5th " Chaflin's Farm 63
" 6th " " " 61
" 54th Mass. Inf., Fort Wagner, 58 ··

The regiments having more than fifty men killed during their period of service are as follows:

Seventy-ninth U. S. C. T.	Total Killed,		183
Eighth	"	"	115
Fourth			102
Thirteenth			86
Seventh			84
Twenty-third	"		82
Sixth			79
Fifth			77
Twenty-second	"		70
First			67
Forty-ninth	··	··	59

Sometimes a comparison will illustrate better than figures alone. I give a single instance: Every one has heard of the charge of the Light Brigade, at Balaklava. I will put beside it a Black Brigade of about the same number of men.

Here they are:

Duncan's Brigade, comprising the Fourth and Sixth Regiments at New Market Heights, Had 683 Lost 365 Percent 53.7
Light Brigade, Balaklava, " 673 " 247 " 36.7

Excess in Duncan's Brigade, 10 118 17

Sanford B. Hunt, M. D., late surgeon of U. S. Volunteers, made an exhaustive research into the capacity of the Negro as a soldier. As to his—

1. Aptitude for drill.
2. Capacity for marching.
3. Endurance of fatigue and hunger.
4. Powers of digestion and assimilation.
5. Immunity from or liability to disabling diseases.

All of which points are treated with great detail, and summed up as follows:

"For the purposes of the soldier he has all the physical charac-
teristics required, his temperament adapts him to camp life, and his
morale conduces to discipline. He is also brave and steady in
action. In all subsequent wars the country will rely largely upon
its Negro population as a part of its military power."

Under the act of Congress passed July 12, 1862, the President
of the United States was authorized to have prepared, with suitable
emblematic devices, Medals of Honor to be presented in the name of
the Congress to such soldiers as should most distinguish themselves
by their gallantry in action and other soldierly qualities. So chary
has the Government been in their issue that the award has not
reached two thousand among the three millions of volunteers and
regulars in the Army and Navy. So that these medals are more rare
than the "Victoria Cross" of England, the "Iron Cross" of Germany,
or the "Cross of the Legion of Honor" of France.

I copy the list of those issued to Negro soldiers as they stand
upon the records, that is, in the numerical order of the regiments
to which the recipients belonged. It will be therefore understood
that this order does not indicate priority of time or degree
of excellence.

Christian A. Fleetwood,	Sergeant Major,	Fourth U. S. C. T.
Alfred B. Hilton,	Color Sergeant,	" "
Charles Veal,	Corporal,	"
Milton M Holland,	Sergeant Major,	Fifth
James Brownson,	First Sergeant,	"
Powhatan Beatty,	First Sergeant,	
Robert Pinn,	First Sergeant,	"
Thomas R. Hawkins,	Sergeant Major,	Sixth
Alexander Kelly,	First Sergeant,	" "
Samuel Gilchrist,	Sergeant,	Thirty-sixth "
William Davis,	Sergeant,	" "
Miles James,	Corporal,	
James Gardner,	Private,	" "
Edward Ratcliffe,	First Sergeant,	Thirty-eighth "
James Harris,	Sergeant,	" "
William Barnes,	Private,	" "
Decatur Dorsey,	Sergeant,	Thirty-ninth "

After each war, of 1776, of 1812, and of 1861, history repeats
itself in the absolute effacement of remembrance of the gallant deeds
done for the country by its brave black defenders and in their rele-
gation to outer darkness.